THE PEOPLE WHO LOOKED DOWN ON ME HELPED ME TO SMILE

Andre Stewart
The People Who Looked Down On Me Helped Me To Smile

Published by BooxAi
ISBN: 978-965-578-755-9

The People Who Looked Down On Me Helped Me To Smile

Andre Stewart

CONTENTS

WHO IS WITHOUT SIN?

Sarah holds in nothing; she talks about everything. I swear he was gonna hit her. He raised his hand like he would. I saw it and gasped out loud like a scene in a dramatic movie. Doesn't he know that Mr. Jones will punish him again? I thought to myself and right when you'd think his fist was going to connect to her face it just dropped. The way that it did, it reminded me of a bird falling from the sky rapidly after being shot. It fell to his side, and she smiled. However, it wasn't of any good as it was really of bad intentions, and I could tell. My uncle Mr. Jones favors his little daughter and I know sometimes that he buys into her stories more than her brother's. She is the apple of her father's eye. The obvious favorite but he would disagree if you asked him. I don't live here, but I am not a stranger. Sometimes living in a house, I could see where I would be like a stranger to someone who's not used to having me around regardless of being family or not. That's just how life is. However, Sarah runs to tell my uncle everything even when it isn't a big deal. Mr. Jones buys apple and orange juices for the house, and I have some then when he comes home, she runs to tell him that I drank some of the juice. Obviously, he says nothing because at the end of the day in reality it isn't a big deal. To 6-year-old Sarah it is. I don't like her just to make that clear and if that sounds a little too harsh, she may be improving at having a better personality and I don't want to be around her to find out. Whichever one sounds best to you. Her brother is far different though. As a matter of fact, sometimes I can't believe that the two are related. Caleb is a chill 10-year-old dude. If I had a choice, I would rather take money being his guardian for the time and not have to deal with Sarah. I keep telling myself it's because she's 6 years old. However, I remember that some people have been miserable, mischievous and manipulative as kids and they are still that way as adults. Promiscuous, poor parents and prideful. Some things just never change. Then I think to myself that Sarah may never change and that she will be just like that forever even as an adult and for the next 6 months that I'm in New York I'll have to deal with her. That scares me but deep down a part of me feels like I might be overreacting. Caleb balances things out. He takes up small responsibilities in the house, doesn't misbehave or acts like a menace. He is basically what you'd consider a good kid to be. The thing is he acts as if he's too grown for his age and if you ask me, I wouldn't say that it's necessarily a bad thing because he doesn't go about it in a disrespectful way. He knows how to keep a conversation going and can add to it. In my opinion, I think he's smart, his academic consistency supports that belief and I'm impressed that in his spare time he chooses to read the books his father owns in the study. Sometimes you'll forget that the boy is even in the house. I don't remember being this way at 10 years old, I was a straight up menace, however, if he sticks to what he is doing now and applies himself, I think that in the next 10 to 15 years he will find himself at a really good place in life that a young man would want to be in. However, his sister pulls him out of his natural element far too often and I think the real reason I get paid to be their guardian when my uncle is not around is to keep one away from the other but still have them spend time together as siblings. It's like a mountain you climb that has occasional good views, but for a part of the ascension you are drenched in rainwater.

As good of a kid as he is, Caleb will fight you if you push his buttons just enough.

 As smart as he is, he hasn't figured out how to hold his anger in for too long. His father is the same way I might add. However, Caleb will try his best though his temperament absorbs bad energy too quickly. When he cools down, we talk, and I'm not surprised that he understands and comprehends the perspective I try to show him. One day I gave him a little exercise to do. I made him walk around the house both upstairs, downstairs and outside holding an egg cuffed safely in between both of his palms.

"Walk slowly," I said to him, and he listened, with obvious curiosity pacing back and forth throughout his mind. I could see. He went up the stairs, downstairs, in the garage, on the porch and in the backyard again where I sat waiting for him carefully holding the egg. We took out the egg tray.

"Why did I have to do that?" He asked.

"Think of yourself as an egg," I said to him,

"Going about life like you did walk around the house carefully guarding your peace of mind. If you rushed or someone made you feel worked up, you'd lose concentration, and the egg would fall and break. No matter who it is, never let someone steal your joy to the point where you crack and break then do something stupid. It's not worth it." I said to him, I imagine saying the same thing to my kids one day and the type of dad I'd become. It ran through my mind in that split second.

I remember one day I took my cousins for a walk in the park, just to get out of the house because it was very much a nice sunny day outside. It was an enjoyable experience for a little bit but then Sarah yanked on Caleb's tail again. They were on the swings, and I don't know what Sarah said to him because even afterwards neither of them would say, but I suspect it wasn't something he wanted to hear her say. I was sitting on the bench watching them when it happened then out of nowhere, I heard him yell at her to stop. She laughed in his face then he got off his swing, pushed her out of the one that she was in and gave her one big punch in the eye. I got up immediately, surprised and furious at the fact he did that. I ran over to them, pulled him off her and with his skinny figure he fell easily onto the grass.

Hey! I shouted.

You don't hit your sister! You don't hit girls at all! I said and then immediately I had to calm down because he gave me eyes he would give his father and I suspected that he thought that I was going to take my belt off and spank him.

"Get up." I then calmly said, changing my tone of voice as I outstretched my hand to help him onto his feet.

His sister's eyes were not looking the best. The bruise around her right eye became swollen and it made them look purple. I rushed them both home right away, icing Sarah's eyes while providing a remedy to ease some of the pain. As I did, Caleb sat facing a corner of the living room in dead silence and sobbing regret. After taking care of his sister, I went over to speak with him.

"Did you forget everything that I told you about the egg?" I asked.

"No cousin." He responded softly.

"I tried to ignore her but I lost it. I'm sorry." He said.

I accepted his apology and we all kind of moved on from that afternoon occurrence. However, when his father came home, he definitely got a serious spanking that I'm sure he won't ever forget for the rest of his life. Maybe he could still feel the pain of his punishment even to this day. I could hear the screams and crying that night and I kind of felt sorry but not so sorry at the same time for him. Maybe this way he could learn from his mistakes.

After that episode, Sarah took a break from being nagging and when she isn't nagging she is actually a very sweet, well behaved and helpful young lady. I think I prefer that version of her more than the crabby one. As the summer was beginning to draw to a close a consistent forecast perplexed upstate. It rained as the temperatures dropped for about a week straight. There were no walks to the park, playing in the backyard or enjoyment of the big yard space that my uncle's house boasted. Then finally, the last week of August blessed us all with some sunshine again. The kids were excited to say the least. That Monday a little after noon we started off to the park easily. In that neighborhood, the residents aren't usually the type to be outside, or doing much. Most if not all the people that live here stay inside and you'll pretty much see them if you go to their house or if you pass them on their way driving out. Nobody stands on corners, plays loud music or behaves like they do where I'm from. It always amazes me how different parts of the world operate. However, as we got closer to the park, I realized an older BMW model parked at the side of the road with its bonnet up. One I haven't honestly seen in quite some time. The color was a bright silver you couldn't miss from a distance as the driver had the headlights on. Both doors were open wide on the passenger and driver side but I didn't see anyone just yet. We were somewhat of a distance away still but really not that far. I thought it odd but brushed it back into my subconscious. As we came closer, a mixed curvaceous woman with decent height popped up from the trunk area of the vehicle in the blink of an eye.

"Excuse me sir." She called out to me and I answered.

"Can you help me with something?" she asked. Apparently according to what I understood from what she was saying an unusual sound was coming from her vehicle and she was unsure of what it was and it made her uncomfortable continuing her journey onward so she decided to stop and check it out. Her words were fast as if it was rehearsed. As she explained, the kids stood and looked nearby from the sidewalk. I could see them, I remember clearly that they weren't far away. The park was in the background, maybe a stone's throw. I proceeded to tell the woman to start her car to see if I could figure out what the issue might be and if I could help her. I'm no mechanic, I thought to myself, I should've told her to call one. However, I brushed that thought in the back of my mind too and figured if I was in some sort of pickle I'd love the help anywhere that I could get it. She started the car and it sounded fine to me. I listened keenly to see if I would hear an inconsistency from the engine or if anything out of the ordinary would pop up but nothing did. She then called my attention to examine the engine itself as she felt in her mind that there must've been an issue with it. We were standing at the driver's side, and the kids watched. I went around the car to its front and examined the engine carefully and it was so totally fine in my eyes. As I looked at the motor, I heard a vehicle approaching nearby.

"Take a look at this here." The woman said then quickly grabbed both my hands firmly with hers talking in an unusually louder tone than she was speaking before. I looked at her wildly. At the same time, I heard Sarah scream.

It was a setup!

I pushed the lady off with all my strength and she fell to the ground hard then took off. I ran around the vehicle and a man was trying to grab a hold of Sarah to take her with him while another watched from the driver's seat in an old van that had pulled up on us. When he saw me running towards him at full speed he immediately let go and started at the van cowardly. I could sense it in his demeanor. White male, short, skinny arms and legs that one could snap in two easily. Caleb tried fighting him off and that's good but he's a kid so his efforts weren't enough to ward off the man. He stopped trying when he saw me coming towards him madly and the man almost got away running.

Bam!

I leaped and dropped him hard too. Then in no time I was on his case.

Left! Right! One step! Two steps!

Punches and kicks flying all over the place. He started to bleed in no time. From the van out stepped the other fella who tried coming to his partner's defense and I got on his short stubby case too.

Left! Right! One step! Two steps! They both got it.

I remember being so mad, I reached for my pocket knife that I always carried in my waist since high school days and just as I was about to jam it in the side of his neck I heard Caleb scream at me.

"No cousin stop!" It was as if something overcame me and I snapped out of it. Quickly, they all made an attempt to drive off in the van and the old silver bmw stayed parked in its spot. I got a good read of the license plate though before they did and as I caught my breath I called the police and filed a report and left the matter in their hands.

Mr. Jones came in later that night from his shift at the hospital and even though he wasn't pleased with what happened he was very much grateful that things turned out the way it did and that I was there. I felt the same and as the temperatures cooled down of what was very much an eventful day Caleb came over to where I sat on the couch and I never forget he looked at me and questioned why I acted as if I wanted to end the man's life.

"You won't understand until you get older," I said to him, knowing deep down within myself that I was actually discomposed at the fact that I allowed myself to get that mad and he saw. He brushed it off as I expected. I never forgot.

"No cousin. I understand just fine." He said to me,

"Maybe you need to start practicing the things that you preach."

Just one of those days?

My eyes open wide as a new day begins. I'm ready to face the world, kinda, sort of and not really. I wish deep down inside I felt better than this. I play some music from Bob Marley to distract me while I get ready. I look in the mirror and I see my whole past, present and future in the blink of an eye. A part of me that makes me feel happy and another part I feel uncertain about. I try to remind myself that it will all be okay if I could just make it through today, I don't need to worry about tomorrow. Tomorrow is not right now.

I've got this!

The world comes at me when I get out of my comfort zone and I feel like things still aren't going the way that I would want them to be. It makes my mind wonder wildly what else could be coming next. However, some part of me is reminded to try and stay cool. Tomorrow will be a better day and whatever is going on right now will be somewhat forgotten. I hold onto that hope even if tomorrow turns out to be even worse than today is. I'm not thinking about that. Tomorrow is not right now. I live in my head a lot on days like this and I take note of the little things. Then there are times that I don't appreciate the little things enough. Whatever and whoever it may be. It's just a part of life and we as people are not perfect. We go through it. Whatever we do to make it through we do it and sometimes we can't think too much about what the people of the world think. The people of the world are not me. They don't go through what I go through as a person and they don't care in the same way that I care. I refuse to let their energy pull me down. I hold onto hope and faith in my life to keep me going. I didn't go in front of the world and tell them that I am perfect. I just try to do what I have to do. I understand that problems with people are never truly gonna go away because you can't make everyone happy. Today some people say this and tomorrow they say something different. Sometimes I can't even control who decides to have a problem with me. You can't please people.

Carry that with you throughout your life on days you possibly might forget. Like one of those days that aren't the best. Yeah, It's just one of those days.

Can't Give Up

Deep down inside I know that I am a strong person. I try to be. Even when it's hard and it feels like there's no way out, I know that I won't choose to live on my knees, I'd rather die standing on my own two feet. If I have a chance to, I will never choose anything but peace, love and happiness. I will choose freedom and life over death. I have to believe this, I'd rather to. For all the times I've helped when I need help the most sometimes the familiar faces are not there. It makes you little by little give up on the people you might've really thought of differently from everyone else. It's hard, but I expect it with many other things in life. I try not to be surprised. Even when it ain't sunny, I'm not going to complain.

I'm not trying to find perfection out of life. I'd rather spend my time doing the little things trying to find the strength and motivation to push through. I have to.

I believe that is one of the most valuable things. A peace of mind.

So many people have a road paved for them effortlessly and they still choose to do nothing with it. Time and time again I live to see so many people have life a little bit better than so many who don't and they make nothing of it. They instead complain the most. I've lost friends, family, had days of financial emptiness, and days when I feel like giving up on everything that I've spent so much time building. Through it all I have to find some strength to tell myself " come on we've got to keep moving. I just can't give up now."

EXCUSE MY UNEASY PEACE OF MIND.

Appreciate the fact that I'm on my own journey. It doesn't have to be all that you approve of. I'd respect your appreciation from a distance if possible. Saying no to you is what you perceive as being rude but what if it meant saying yes to myself? Would it really be all about you then? Love and loyalty can be questionable when some people show it because you have to ask yourself if they mean what they're saying sometimes. it's like you have to always try to put it to the test. I wrestle with myself at the expense of my peace of mind and at the end of the day I feel drained. I have very little energy left to show for all the time I spent in my head overthinking things. Some people don't help either. Guilt trip, entitlement and trying to prove like you're too real of a person stinks. I see you and I'm getting an understanding of what you're about. Your words are so empty it's unattractive. Why do you take the time out of your day to talk to me?

Jeez!

I wish someone else who matched your energy would come along so you could move along. Somewhere sometime, just not right here and not right now. I'm not trying to listen to all your problems when I'm trying to figure out solutions on my own and usually that's all you've got to talk about. All the problems that's in your life. It's hard to see the positive with the way that you bring certain things to perspective. It's like you've given up hope and I don't like that. Perhaps I'm the one who's running away from the fact that sometimes I feel that way too and I don't like to be reminded of it. Who honestly wants to be reminded of the bad things that they already know about themselves through other people anyways? I'm working on it, trying to fix it and it takes time and work. I don't need you to make me feel bad when I think about it. Not right here, not right now. Even though I go through rough times in my life they've never heard me say the things that I've heard them say. They take reality for granted and think what they see is how it is all the time. Just give it time and you'll realize real soon that they'll start to try and write your own stories for you and tell you what to do with your life. However, it'll always be a problem if you ever told them what to do on their own. I'm not here to spoil you, don't expect anything from me. You have your reality and I have mine.

Nobody has hurt me as much as you do.

Smile today, spread the love and have some joy in your life. Be happy for your own sake. I'm trying to find this thing called peace of mind and it took me a while. Living in your head and thinking too much about things doesn't help. It's a beautiful morning, the songbirds flash by my eyes and I can hear them sing sweetly. The luscious Blue Mountains connect with the sky in such a way that you'll realize that there are no clouds. Jamaica is beautiful. I can breathe, I can hear, I can smell and I can stand on my own two feet. Thank God that I am well. I love myself for who I am today and who I was yesterday and for whoever I will be tomorrow no matter how things turn out. That's a promise. Believe me when I tell you that I live with regrets. Memories creep into my mind about some things that I wish I could've handled differently and then I begin to hate every-thing about myself. I guess I was hoping things would turn out perfect but I didn't understand at one point in time that no such thing exists. When you compare yourself to people, you set unrealistic goals, and everything that you have around you sometimes you may view as completely useless. These things do happen.

What are you gonna tell me? You can't tell me anything that I haven't heard before! I don't listen!

I don't ask questions and I blame you and them for my mistakes. Who am I? Just the guy who looks in the mirror after all this time to realize that the person looking back has hurt me more than anyone else could ever do.

DUPPY

"They say duppy a come! You better sleep with the Bible under your pillow before you go to bed tonight and cover up under your blanket."

I watched her lips as she talked and at the same time I saw Shakeem let out a big laugh so I laughed too.

Rema is hot today, and there is not even one cloud in the sky to spare the troubles that this heat brings. We're on summer break and not much is going on these days. It felt like we were way better off just staying in school. Our parents definitely agreed. They couldn't wait for us to get out of the house again. They tell us we're eating up too much of the food that's in the house. However, they'd rather see the food go to waste. I know. We are sitting on the park benches watching John crows chase the sky, as well as playing cards and making fun of each other as time goes along. Sierra is the jokester , Shakeem is the quiet one and William as well as I entertain her jokes. Sometimes but not all the time. William is a little boy, his mother, brother, sisters and relatives all live in England so his only family in Jamaica is his grandmother with whom he lives with. The little boy basically has no friends and we kind of keep up his energy and try to keep him in good spirits. It's the least that we could do for our neighbor. I can't imagine what life would be like growing up as an only child. I'm so happy I have siblings to share my life with.

Sierra loves to joke around William though a little too much to the point where I believe that the boy thinks it's literal. It's funny and not so funny sometimes but he is also 7 years old. If you should tell him that the cow jumps over the moon he will probably believe you. I feel sorry for him sometimes, but I know that he will grow out of it one day and we will all sit down and have a laugh about it I hope. I remember one day one of the elders in our community, Mr. Marlon who basically has lived in Trench town his whole life saw us in the park one day playing cards and decided to join us. A couple of years before now he was more of a chubby man, however since he retired from the police force he got really skinny. Some people say he's diabetic and some people say he's stressed but I never decided to ask. People gain weight today and lose it tomorrow, that's just how life is. One day Mr. Marlon was cruising down Collie smith street and saw us over by the park listening to music and playing cards so he stopped by to chit chat and ended up playing a few rounds of cards with us. As we played we talked and the conversation never really stuck on one thing for too long. It kind of just flowed until Mr. Marlon said something that triggered the little boy and William tried to debate the big man.

"I don't believe you," William said and it's like I saw Marlon's eyebrows raised so high in curiosity and eyes of wonder.

"Little boy!" Marlon said in a deep voice and we all started to pay attention more then.

"Ghosts are real! Listen to what I'm telling you and don't let anyone take you for a fool. I've seen a duppy already." He says.

"Madness!" The little boy responds in poise and in complete disbelief. For as young as he is he rocks a grown man's attitude and I feel like Marlon realizes that and maybe some place deep inside of his mind feels threatened by it. However, I could be wrong.

"Look over there." He says and points to May Pen cemetery on Spanish Town road. William looks as he does so.

"One night I came in after drinking in town by myself and I walked through the cemetery yard to come home." Marlon begins.

"It was almost midnight and you could only see a few cars driving on the street. I had no money left and I spent my last few dollars on beers at the bar. Out of nowhere!" Marlon jumps emphatically out of the seat as we all watch with smiles in our face's listening carefully.

"When I was walking, out of nowhere I saw a bright-white figure slowly approaching me from a distance. I made nothing of it until it came up real close. It was a white man." He said then we all gasped. In the neighborhood that we grew up in rarely do you see a white person walking about. They don't come to this side of Jamaica just to hang around.

"Are you sure?" I asked him curiously and then he looked me in my eyes and said to me "I swear to God."

" I became frightened." He continued. "But the white man told me not to be scared." When he said that we all laughed out loud again.

"The man told me he got lost and that he needed directions to some hotel by the airport downtown so I told him." Marlon said. As he talked he used his hands as gestures.

"I tried to look into his eyes but I could see nothing. All I could see was a dark blank space. He didn't even have any sensible clothing, just a long white sleeve t-shirt that looked so clear that it must've been heavily bleached." As he talked we all tried to picture it in our minds but I can't speak for everyone else but I definitely had trouble doing so. As active as my imagination was, I still couldn't picture a white man walking through May pen cemetery at 12 o'clock at night. However, Marlon continued.

"After I told the man where to find his hotel the man grabbed my hand, shook it and put three thousand dollars in my right pocket." Instantly we saw the elder pull out some crushed up notes all adding up to three thousand Jamaican dollars he said that the duppy gave him.

"Woah!" I heard William exclaim and I thought to myself yep, he's already sold on Mr. Marlon's story.

"After he gave me the money." Marlon continued.

"I saw the man run away so fast I could never imagine the fastest man in the world running like that. He just disappeared." He said.

"When I looked around I couldn't see him in the distance. He had to be a ghost." William hissed his teeth as Marlon finished talking. It traveled with the little breeze that went to war with the blazing heat.

"Man you're talking nonsense," William said. "I can't believe y'all are listening to this grown man talk this garbage." The little boy said, then he got up and just walked away from us all. Look who decided to come to terms with reality. I thought to myself.

"We should prank him," Sierra said and Mr. Marlon agreed.

"Nah, that wouldn't be nice," I said, disagreeing with the two of them.

"Don't you think that the kid has been through enough in his life?" I added.

"So what?" Sierra asked and then the both of them looked at me waiting for a response that I didn't have right away. I thought about it in my head for a little and then I said ah what the hell, he's 7. How much harm could we really do? I thought to myself.

The next day came along and we sat In the park again playing cards. This time it was just me, Shakeem, Sierra and the little boy William. Ever since yesterday Sierra made it a point of duty to try and talk to William about ghosts to try and make fun out of the situation.

" I believe in ghosts, man. I see them all the time." She would say to him in a comedic way.

"Leave me alone. You guys are stupid. There are no such things as ghosts." He would respond. Me and Shakeem would laugh on the inside and continued playing the game but saying nothing. All along Sierra would find a way to say something just to scare him but he would always shut her down.

"You're crazy or You're talking madness." William would say completely denying anything that the girl troubled him about. We waited patiently and finally the perfect time came around. All four of us Marlon, Sierra, Shakeem and I decided to get some old clothing, some markers and red dye as well as a prop knife. Our plan was to have the old man dress up and look like the chucky doll but the Jamaican version, so we got him some fake dreadlocks and gave him red contacts to put in his eyes. I liked that he tagged along with the idea. If he was younger he would have definitely won some sort of Halloween costume contest if you asked me. He looked scary enough and we all found it funny. During the day we set up a plan to go to William's house that night when it was predicted that there would be a full moon. Every chance that we took we, but mainly Sierra, made fun of him and tried to scare him by talking about ghosts again. During this time the old man was at home preparing himself for the grand entrance. Despite his age, he is definitely young at heart.

"Nobody can't scare me!" William boasted again and again. To our amusement. The day progressed eventually and the night time approached. We all took our time walking home from the park and convinced the kid that we would stop by his house for a little bit before we all went home to our separate ways. As expected there was no push back in that regard and we all walked to William's and sat on his veranda talking. It was all a part of the plan.

We sat there for a little while until, out of nowhere, the lights to his house started to flicker on and off until bam! They shut off completely.

"What's going on, I asked?" In a concerning but not so concerning way to him. His grandma wasn't home just yet from work and it was just us kids.

"That's odd. I don't know." William said as he rose from his feet to go inside the house to check on some of the light switches. We watched and from the back of the house Sierra gave Marlon the cue to sneakily go in. He did, and as he did all our hearts pounded with excitement.

"Oh, there's nothing wrong, it just seemed as if the breaker might've switched off accidentally," William uttered. As he said that we watched him from the front of the yard flip the switch then boom, all of the lights in the house turned right back on. Then little William got a tap on his shoulder.

"Wanna play?"

The little boy turned round frantically, and there was Mr. Marlon standing right behind him with a prop knife raised, dressed spookily with fake blood all over his face as well as his clothing.

"Aaah!" I heard the little boy scream in terror and immediately we all laughed. In literally the blink of an eye he peed his pants so bad it soaked his trousers and Sierra was right there to catch it all on camera.

YES SAH

In the words of a great man;

"Buy me some ganja for my Christmas present then wrap it up neatly and put it under my Christmas tree. I promise even if I tell you that's what I want when I get it I will act astonished. Tis the season right?" He said.

Another spliff roll, but you dare not try and give that to no Rastafarian. The rasta man has his chalice and it's lit. A chunk load of smoke escapes his lungs through his nostrils and I'm always amazed at how the smoke looks like a whole universe that we haven't experienced. Food for thought. Always try to remember that nobody is perfect. A man that sits down and watches the things that's going on in the world can tell you a lot about life more than someone who is busy everyday going about and is a part of the hassle. I realized taking it easy sometimes is one of the best things that you could ever do for yourself and your health because this world has a tendency to stress you and eat you up alive. Sometimes it feels like there are not enough hours in the day. Life really comes at you fast. I think about it so much that it gives me anxiety and then I start to worry. I worry about the things that I can't control and I worry about how I could've done the things that I've already done a little bit better. I wish I was not such a perfectionist. I wish I didn't have to always have things done in a perfect way. Perhaps I feel as if it wouldn't work out for me any other way if I didn't try to make it the best. Then I look at life and realize that they're some people out there who make it without even trying. I won't say that life is unfair. I don't blame life for the things that take place all the time. I just understand taking things for what they are and just leaving it at that. I've been around some people in my life and have friends who think like me and deal with anxiety sometimes on a bigger level for things that I probably wouldn't let bother me but I'm not in their shoes. Everyone is different. What may bother me doesn't bother them and vice versa. I don't believe that drugs are the answer to your problems, but I know so many people who blaze the herb just to keep mellow and irie. I don't blame them. Some people commit suicide. I know that nobody can truly smoke their problems and pain away but I understand sometimes having a higher meditation can give you answers as well as solutions to the same problems that you might've not thought of before. It's true. I don't judge people. I never could tell what someone is going through in their life and why they drink and smoke the way they do. I just try to give a listening ear and not put myself in their problems or be too concerned about what they plan to do. I know a lot of people who get locked up for a plant that grows in the ground and they use it recreationally. It always amazes me how one side of society looks down on something that another side of society appreciates and uses everyday. Maybe the people who make the rules one day will change their minds when it affects them or the people in their circle. Who knows? It could get better or it could get worse.

"Yes sah!"

"Marijuana is God's gift to earth." I heard Kevin say. His dreadlocks are as tall as a broomstick and he wears them proudly. Nobody could ever kill his vibe.

Don't kill my vibe

Some people don't have an actual reason as to why they dislike you. A real explanation is just not there. As a matter of fact, if the opportunity should ever present itself, they'll find the most minuscule thing to use and bury you alive then tell people proudly what they really think of you. Seriously. I could care less about changing the way some people really feel on the inside. I told myself that it just won't work. From me to them the bridge is slowly falling down and I don't have a real issue with it. I try to find happiness either way. That's something I learned from my father, mother and grandmother too. Don't ever let somebody steal your joy. No matter what it may be. Just go ahead and turn that frown upside down and go about life differently and spread the love with the people you meet. Before you say something bad to somebody it's better if you don't say anything at all. Hold your words and preserve your attitude because it'll probably just not amount to nothing anyways but you being worked up. I know sometimes it's hard, because there are times when I just honestly want to say what's on my mind and truly air my feelings out but I hold my own self back. Maybe I'm still taking the feelings of others into consideration or I'm seeing how certain things could work out before it even does and it wouldn't look too good. Maybe for my own sake too in the long run, it's better that some things I try not to say. The people that live in a bubble can't handle that. It's really not about them, it's really for me. There's no telling what someone who is delusional and has power will do and sometimes, you will never see it coming and that hurts you the most. Sometimes in some ways that you can't even understand, it just happens. In my life I understand that abusing power is a very dangerous thing. People will believe what they don't take time to find out. If someone associates something in their environment as bad and doesn't take time to actually know what it is they will always be ignorant to it and curse you every day about it.

Ding! Dong!

The doorbell rings and a familiar face is behind it. A smirk turns into a smile that seconds later transforms into a laugh. A tall black skinhead.

"What's up playa?" We greet each other.

"The only thing changing is the weather." He says to me, at the same time he presents me with a bag that's neatly wrapped up in another bag that's all put together in a burger king bag. Then, before he forgets he reaches for a soda cup. It's heavy and it smells good and I bet you some money that it won't spill over. We talk for a little bit, not even two minutes, and then I see "her" pull into the driveway. Her kids were in the back, and I could feel her eyes watching us from across the street.

"Damn why people here gotta be so nosy." I thought to myself. I change the topic between me and my guest and he gets the drift. We shake hands and then he leaves before she even gets out of the car. I like to call her Miss Neighborhood watch. She's an "outcast" just like me, which makes many things very interesting. I say good morning to her and she fights to say it back in a measly tone that you wouldn't even talk to your dog. I've only moved here for 3 months, I'm not moving with the intention of having problems with people but sometimes things in life do happen. If you should've asked me then and asked me right now I'd tell you I have absolutely no idea why Miss neighborhood watch has a problem with me. There is none. I keep telling myself maybe she just doesn't like the fact that we are neighbors. However, this lady doesn't pay my rent and I'm pretty sure she can agree that there's never been any disrespect from my end to hers. I have no clue what the real problem is. I've learned that apparently she's telling the other neighbors my music is too loud and eroded with profanity, my tattoos should be covered up and I am way too unGodly. She's learned this from across the street and is not even next door to me. I scratch my head at the thought because my neighbors next door have something completely different to say and it's positive. As a matter of fact they're way closer to me than she is. I didn't confront her about it, but there were some days when I felt like I should've. However, there are some days I'm happy that I didn't. Some things I prefer to leave in the hands of time. I saw her one day snooping around in another neighbor's backyard and from what I saw it looked like she may be picking a fruit off their tree. As she did, she made sure to keep her eyes peeled over my yard looking at me. I was in the back minding my own business unwinding with a spliff so big it looked like a pencil. I saw her, but I saw her too late. She didn't show herself up again but instead watched from the living room window everytime that I got a delivery. I could feel her watching, and it felt uncomfortable but I didn't feel as if I was worried but rather more concerned about what she might do with what she knows. I wondered when she would've figured out that her son hides to do the same thing too. It was one of those things at that point in my life that ridiculed me. I'm not a stranger to hate, and I can tell differently when I feel like that energy is around me versus when it's not. It ridiculed me because there's nothing that she could've said that would be true that paints me into this terrible person that she is projecting. Maybe I mind my business a little too much, who knows?

I remember one day the doorbell rings and Zion the dog barks and wags his tail excitedly, even though he knows that it's not the mailman.

"What's up playa." I greet my dear friend. Before I could even get my sentences off right I saw the blue lights flashing and the sirens bumping real loud racing from around the corner. Cars from the left, and cars from the right approaching the driveway. I could tell they weren't too far away as if they've been watching.

"Don't move!" They yelled and pretty soon half of the neighbors living on the street were out on their lawns. Everyone wanted to know what all the commotion was about in what usually is a quiet and peaceful neighborhood. They made a scene and as they did I saw "her" come out of the house with a smile tucked neatly away in her facial expression. Damn. I thought as I shook my head.

"What's in the bag?" One of the officers asked my guest and without hesitation he presented the officer with a Subway bag with two foot-long subs inside. The man looked confused. He looked at my guest, looked at me and said nothing. He then proceeded to try and search the house in addition to the car that my guest drove in. To their surprise they found nothing, because nothing was there to begin with. As expected, a measle, drawn out sorry not so sorry apology was given and afterwhile they left.

"Sir, this man is a door dash driver," I said.

"He's just dropping off some food." I knew he felt embarrassed to not find what he was looking for and had me tell him that. Thinking back on it from time to time I laugh, but I look at it differently sometimes in terms of the extent to which people will go to do something to you for no reason. One day you'll be reminded that you don't live in a bubble.

I'M YOUR HERO?

I wish sometimes the world was more of a place where people could be more understanding. How do you expect me to have the same story as everyone else when I'm living a different life? Some people aren't as fortunate as I am and some people are more fortunate than me. For many reasons I feel like it's simple enough for people to understand but easy for people to forget until they find themselves or someone that they know in the same predicament. Life is hard and sometimes I feel like always trying to be a positive person in someone's life could be challenging. It could get draining and you'll break down from time to time in public or behind closed doors battling wars silently that nobody else sees. A lot of people are suffering. We need money but money doesn't always equate to a peace of mind. I don't want to be the same person when I get rich. They're gonna kill me or take advantage of me right in the same neighborhood that I grew up in. In the midst of it all, you will find a lot of the kids will really look up to you. You're gonna be like somebody's hero. In this world they always try to get rid of the heroes and portray them in a bad way. If anybody gets rich or successful just know that it's coming. Sometimes it could even be the people who are your own or in the worst case scenario it could even be our own self. We self-destruct.

Stop lying!

I heard someone respond to me after telling them the same thing the other day. However, A lot of our heroes break down and cry as well as hide their pain through addiction. Reputation, status and money doesn't elude you from an uneasy peace of mind. If your favorite rapper goes through the same thing that you go through maybe you need to stop looking at him like Jesus. Talented and famous, yes. Perfect, no. We all know that but it's like we always forget and we are too big in the chest to even acknowledge. How are you gonna make someone else mad but get mad when they get mad too? How do you not understand? How do you verbally chastise someone everyday for what they have or don't have but feel some type of way when someone judges you? Who do you think you are? A lot of people who have been incarcerated came back out changed their lives and are not the same thinkers as when they made whatever mistake. Why are they disqualified from being somebody's hero? See me as a person, I'm going through life just like you. To the people who love, respect me and appreciate me I am their hero and they are mine. I'm not expecting the people who don't like me to feel the same way and that's ok.

Fear?

What's going on mate? Life isn't always about a bunch of sunshine and roses. Take the good and the bad when it comes and learn to move on and be happy. Not everything lasts forever but if you're alive you've got to learn to move on.

Irie.

A lot of things in life are there naturally because it's supposed to be in that space, don't interfere with it. Do what you want to do and call yourself whatever you want to call yourself but don't run from reality. Life is hard for you and me. I don't expect you to understand and I don't always expect you to see what I'm saying. I expect you to be defensive and try to debate about it so when you do I'm not surprised so I'll try not to even get angry. I promised myself that. I will move along with life. I know what I've said and I've said what I said. It's for a reason. I did not put a gun to your head when I said it. Some people will try to use your own words against you and say you did all kinds of things. The average person and people who are in power. The response is the same, do whatever you want to do. I know that power will never always be in the hands of one person or group of people for too long. I know there are many others out there who feel the same just as I do and maybe they're scared to say it. Maybe people who truly understand haven't come along just yet but when they do the same thing that I've said today or yesterday will be repeated maybe even in a more emphatic way and there will be people who will do things for the greater good against anything that anyone could ever do to me. I have only one life and I mean something to people. There is no way that I should ever allow myself to be afraid. I am who I am and whatever I think I'll ever be afraid of I have to learn to live with that reality whether it's for better or worse. It's a lonely reality with a big responsibility that you will never truly escape from but my life means so much more than whatever or whoever I might be afraid of. If I feel inspired I will speak.

THE ART OF DESTRUCTION?

"Yeah Yeah. Whatever you say." Jenny beckoned teasing Alfred. It's obvious they both like each other, but they're both too shy to admit. However, it's pretty much obvious and others could see. For no other boy does her eyes twinkle in such a special way and for no other girl he gets so nervous and smiles so uniquely. When people are in love it shows. It has a type of feeling and a particular look that can't be faked easily.

"On your mark! Get set! Go!" Michael yelled then in the blink of an eye Alfred and Jenny took off running. When he wasn't going too fast, he wore a grin on his face. He underestimated the girl. His 6 '2 figure glided swiftly through the grass without much effort and Jenny would have to swing her hands and move her feet extra harder just to keep up. They share a love on the track and are always competitive people even though on most occasions Alfred is the one who wins the duel. That doesn't stop Jenny from believing that there will be one day that she will beat him and use that opportunity to brag about it for weeks. She has strong faith and it is commendable, because Alfred would always win the races that they would have. When he was extra in love with her though he may have slowed up or had pretended to have a muscle ache so that she would catch him up and win the race. For the next couple of days he could expect the kids at school asking if Jenny, such a short girl, really beat him at the track. That's how the kids at their school think. Whatever it may look like and whatever people think it's very difficult for them to change how they feel about it. From the young to the old many people always say it is possible but I don't feel like they actually believe it.

A light breeze brushed across their faces as they were nearing the finishing marker.

"I'm coming, I'm gonna catch you!" Jenny said, chasing down Alfred as if she was a lioness closing in on a zebra. The grin that the boy had on his face turned into a humongous laugh. It caused him to slow up and within a split second Jenny passed him quickly winning the race.

"See. I told you I was gonna beat you."

As she said, Alfred stood with hands resting on his knees playing as if he was exhausted, laughing even more. He really liked her and this time again he made her win the race.

"I'm telling you Saturday I'm gonna surprise a lot of people at the track meet." She says to him as they both try to catch their breath.

"Nah you're gonna come in fourth again just like last time." He said.

"No way." She responded "I'm gonna do better this time I can just feel it. I know that I'm ready."

In just a little bit of time their eyes glued to each other gracefully and just when you thought Alfred would take a hint and kiss her he didn't. His shyness got into the way again even though she was really hoping that he would've. At times she puzzles with the thought of trying to be the one to kiss him first but she feels insecure doing so.

"Guys kiss first." She could hear her friends repeat in the back of her mind. It became gospel so it's hard for her to fight that feeling and be too courageous to take that chance and kiss him especially if she feels nervous to begin with. Once again the moment passed.

It just so happened that the grand eventful day began with cool temperatures and a partly cloudy sky that light showers escaped from. Initially, not many people were out in Lucea town, but as time went on the crowd grew in size and momentum. The day of The Boys and Girls Track and Field Western Championships was finally here! Radio personalities, news media and a few celebs were visible. It was a big deal. To the east of the stadium, Jenny and Alfred along with other athletes on the team were getting warmed up and ready to compete in their respective events. For the most part they all seemed confident and in an uplifting mood. After warm ups, coach Franics walked over to speak with his athletes and gave them that much needed extra motivational boost. His strong words of encouragement, aimed to have the athletes in a determined state of mind solely focused on concentration and the determination to put their best effort out. It worked. Mr. Francis is not just a commendable coach but a remarkable person as well. Anyone who is inspired to be great would want someone like him in their corner mentoring them to achieve their goals.

The day's event started with athletes competing in field events such as the shot put, javelin and discus throw. Immediately following the high and long jump events were next and the pole vault concluded all the competitions off the track. At this point in time the light showers eased making way for the sunshine to introduce a bright and energetic feeling to the day. The sprint events were now about to begin. As the athletes traveled from the east point of the stadium, the population in attendance grew favorably. Even the announcers held more of an exciting tone in their voices. It made one feel like something special was about to happen.

"Here's the lineup for the girls 100m dash." The announcer whipped commercially and as they did you could see the girls walking briskly through the tunnel from the warm up area. The big crowd didn't intimidate Jenny. She kept her cool as she always does saying a prayer deep within and holding onto the faith that her best was yet to come. Her eyes were so focused on the finishing line, it's picture worthy. In no time they were all lined up in the blocks, told to get on their marks and in a heartbeat the gun fired with the young ladies sprinting off. Jenny doesn't usually have a fast start but once she gets going there's no stopping her. A much taller girl next to her from Clarendon College took the lead in the early point of the race. It didn't last long though. Here comes Jenny sprinting past her! Quick strides, focused eyes and arms swinging in form. It was as if a little rocket was taking off from earth into the universe. Coach Francis looked on proudly. The rest of the pack were left in the dust and basically all forgotten. The crowd went wild. What a performance! After she crossed the finish line the clock blinked, a new record was set. Alfred looked on from the sidelines happily but more surprised than anything. In that moment he understood clearly that you can't underestimate this thing called girl power. As the stadium continued to erupt with excitement, the competitive spirit he had burned fiercely. Now it was time for the gents to compete and he would get his chance to show Jamaica what he could do. In comparison to his opponents he stood the tallest. If you paid close attention you will see him talking to himself in the blocks mentally coaching himself through a race he was about to run. The art of self-affirmations, he believed in it wholeheartedly.

"You're not winning this race boy! No matter what you say to yourself, forget it. This is my race punk!" A shorter, more muscular wise mouthed lad standing next to Alfred chirped. He was clearly trying to throw Alfred off his concentration and it seemed like it worked.

"You shut the hell up punk! Nobody knows you here, this is my race. I should beat you up right now you little boy." Alfred responded angrily. The official nearby who caught wind of what took place shouted at the two to knock it off and they ceased the chitter chatter.

"On your marks!" As the official embarked on the instructions the fire in the young lads infused emphatically. It was good.

"Get set! Go!"

The gun fired once more and all the boys dashed off. Immediately Alfred's tall figure stepped up in form and positioned himself with the lead in the race. His strong arms swung in form with his long bony legs leading swiftly. He looked like a young Usain Bolt. Just like Jenny, he separated himself from the pack and it was a struggle for 2nd and 3rd. In the end a new record hadn't been broken but it was still an impressive performance. IT made coach Francis look on proudly.

"What have you got to say now punk? Did you see that? You ate my dust." Alfred screamed at the boy energetically. The boy said nothing in return but flipped Alfred off boldly. Alfred grew angry again.

Bam!

Alfred swung a punch at the boy and he fell to the ground immediately like a sack of potatoes.

"Oh no!" One of the prominent commentators beckoned in astonishment as Jamaica looked on. I could imagine the viewers at home gasping in surprise too.

"No Alfred!" Coach Francis called out amidst all the excitement trying to stop the boy from his actions. He looked like he wanted to strike him again. In a hurry the official that stood not far away ran over to the pair to break the fight from escalating. Alfred had made his temperament get the best of him. When he snapped out of it and realized what he had done, he had a bubbling instant regret.

"Number 0365 disqualified." The event announcer spoke on the intercom and after she did the boos echoed from all areas in the crowd. Tears filled his eyes and raced down his cheek uncontrollably. What have I done Alfred asked himself with no answer.

The officials removed him off the track and a big bright smile appeared on the boy who chirped at him.

"Ha Ha!"

The outcome of the situation made it seem as if he won and Alfred had lost but in a different way. The officials brought the tall young man back to the warm up area and coach Francis came to speak with him right after.

"What the hell were you doing out there man?" He said to Alfred.

"You already won the race but you let someone who lost get the better of you. Are you crazy?" He finished.

His words demolished his esteem from the inside out and broke Al's spirit completely. He felt terrible that he didn't do a better job controlling his emotions, especially because someone who couldn't even compete with him was trying to bring him down and in the end got the better of him. How unfortunate.

Not Perfect

I'm here to bless the world with my words. It doesn't matter what he says, she says or what they say. I'm only in control of what I say. The negative agenda that they bring I don't have to reciprocate. Not every comment needs a response. I smile a lot these days, taking the time to rebuild my energy. I'm trying, I promise I'm learning. Each and everyday I try to count my blessings and hold them closely to my heart. There are some days I have to remind myself that I don't need to rely on the things of the world to make me happy. However sometimes when I look too deep within myself and revisit some memories I feel like a lot of unresolved issues get an opportunity to resurface. I distract myself, to help myself let go of the things that were. I distract myself to try to move on. I feel like if I lived and focused too much on the past it would rob me of my present and future self. Sometimes I wish there was an answer for everything in life, but frankly there will not always be one. A lot of discussions in life aren't always easy to actually sit down and have. It's easy for people to judge something and someone that they don't truly understand. It's easy to make fun of the life that someone is living because you might've escaped and don't have to live it anymore or you've never had to deal with any situations like that at all. Be careful. Sometimes it's better to be silent and preserve your words than to rather bring life to your words that carries an unfortunate energy to you or your family. You never know. They say that the stone that the builder refuses will be the head corner stone. They say sometimes that from the worst of communities remarkable, intelligent and talented people who make an impact on society are born. They have their own stories. I pray to God that you take the spirit of discrimination away from me. Let me not judge people for their story because I know so many who can't and will never understand my own.

You're my hero dad

You've helped me to see the world through love. Father's day should not be the only day that you appreciate your dad. I love and appreciate my father for so many things. Even though he can't always be around me I can't think of what my life would've ever been like without him. My love and respect will always go out to you because I know who you are. Thank you for helping me be who I am. I can't thank you enough. I know that things will not always be perfect but you will always be my dad. I hold you in a very special place in my heart and I will always do. When I think about you I'm reminded of someone who's strong minded, determined, humble, loving and caring. You always hoped and prayed for the best for my life. I appreciate you. I know a lot of people who never had a father in their life. I will always appreciate you and make sure to let my kids know what my father truly meant to me. You're my hero dad and you will always be.

To you my mother

Thank you is something you'll always hear me say as well as I love you. You always wanted to see the best for me at every stage in life. Life was hard and I knew that but our family has some very special memories I wouldn't trade for nothing in this world. You made me know what love means through the love that you've given me as your son. You are one of those people that made me understand what having peace of mind is like. I'm sorry for the times when I was younger and ignorant. I'm sorry for the times when I didn't listen. As I get older as a young man I understand what it means to have a meaningful woman in your life. Someone who has your back. I know for sure that my mom has my back and will always have my back. I'm her boy and I will always be her boy. That is something I know that when I think about brings me internal happiness and peace of mind. I wish I always understood how to appreciate time to the best of my ability so that I knew how to love and treasure someone. I feel like my generation is losing their core. They are losing their morale as well as values and are becoming self centered people. A lot of them complain when they get hurt doing the same thing that they did to people. I have to interact with them, in my world there's no way that I would miss them. Not even by a stretch of the imagination. Even if you aren't very much of a rude talking disrespectful person, being around some of these kids will make you want to be that type of person sometimes. Then the influence of my uneasy peace of mind kicks in and then I do something that my mother wouldn't approve of. That my parents wouldn't approve. It's hard to be the bigger man and walk away sometimes. I don't always want that to be my identity because sometimes I feel like I want to stand up and fight. In my own mind I battle with the things that I want others to like and approve about me as well as what I actually need to do for myself. I am my mother's child so I am going to be sometimes under the influence thinking like my mother would. However, that doesn't stop me from being who I am. I know that my mom loves me unconditionally for it. There is no hate. This brings me peace of mind. I am still her boy. Sometimes I make mistakes and do things she wouldn't approve of but I know there's always going to be love there. Thank you to my mother for showing me that.

To my kids

Y es! I aspire to have kids one day and this is what I plan to say to them:

I love to see your mother get ready for work in the morning. She's sexy. You have a good mother and I promise I wouldn't set you up for failure. Respect her, love and cherish her. Never take any moment for granted even if it's not always how you planned it. Take love with you, it's the only way you'll achieve a lot of things to this thing called life. Believe in yourself, bet on yourself and take risks. You never really know how far you can really get. I see the world when I look into your eyes and that makes me proud. To my kids I love you always remember that in good times and in bad times you're my favorite. I wouldn't trade anything or anyone for you and I would give my life for yours. I've already seen the world and now it's your turn. Make of it what you may but never run from the facts. Stand on it. If it is what it is, don't trip. Never let people make you lose yourself. Take God with you and ask him questions. Believe in his answers even if you think they're not the best, just wait until time tells everything. I hope you find this peace of mind that money can't bring. I hope you love yourself because you love yourself and not because of what people like about you. People don't even like themselves and that doesn't really help. I want you to motivate yourself and set goals so high even if the world doesn't think that you can achieve it. Don't worry about that. Telling yourself that you can do something is better than doing nothing and telling yourself that you don't need to do anything. Don't be lazy. Work smart and work harder. Count your dollars and put them away for a rainy day. Never put the value of people too high that it affects the way that you think about yourself. Love yourself. Find happiness and when you find it cherish it. Don't let any and everybody all up in your space. Try to be aware of everything and don't take anything for granted. I really hope life turns out the way you planned it and I hope you know that you're the best thing that ever happened to my life.

BETTER MUST COME

I'm sure someone somewhere that you mean well will tell people that you're a wicked person. At this point in my life I've just learned to accept it. To live and go through the world sometimes you have to learn to put up with a lot of things that you might not deem comfortable for a little while. If you want to go far, you'll need to stay consistent with the things that you do. Consistency at times can be very much of a challenging experience because the journey will not always be an easy one. Leaning on your faith that you'll make it through requires a strong mind, and a diligent heart that some people just don't have. If it takes ten or twenty years, the goal and the objective won't ever change. You don't get to your dreams by just doing some work today and expecting to see the results tomorrow. It's something that you have to do every day. Believe that within yourself if you don't believe anything else. I'm here for a purpose or else I wouldn't have been here. Nobody can take my spot and make me feel threatened. Everything that I have was never because of what you decided to give me. I worked for this. Sometimes people don't see the work that you put in yourself but judge you the most. It's like no matter what I say and do, I will always be the bad person in their storyline. They tell people, and I realized some buy into that story. I really shouldn't take time out of my day to correct them but sometimes I do. Deep down for a while it definitely bothered me.

I'm learning to try and find happiness by appreciating the simple things that life has to offer and I know that I am blessed. I want to live a life more free, less depressed and definitely fulfilling. Take your time with everything that you do. There is no rush, because by being patient and consistent life will get better from here and better must come.

EVERYDAY ABOVE GROUND.

Don't ever take birthdays for granted. Go out and enjoy yourself. Everyday above ground is a blessing even in the most unfortunate of situations trying to appreciate life. Don't blame life for what life already is. I don't think we truly understand how fortunate we are and how bad things could actually be. I don't think we truly understand how good God is. A day will come when we will lose our blessings and we will try everything in our power to get it back but it won't work. Don't be ungrateful. So many people leave their houses and will never make it back home. So many people didn't wake up this morning.

Make use of everything because nothing lasts forever. Push yourself to overcome and achieve the things that you want in life. Success doesn't come knocking at your door just like that. For who? For what? Seize today aggressively if you have to. There are people who get up everyday before sunrise to clock in and spend hours just trying to make a dollar or two. I applaud them. They could've been lazy because It's not hard to do nothing.

I don't know where the world will turn in a couple of years from now but I want to take my happiness and peace of mind with me. I feel like it's important. As the body ages, strong bones deteriorate.

The richness of the mind shouldn't be under-appreciated. You can have the world and still be unhappy deep down inside. I've seen it.

Stretch marks are natural. As a matter of fact it's beautiful. Competing with somebody younger than you will drain some of the energy that you have left. One day you'll wake up and realize that it makes no sense.

What you find appealing at 25 is not what you'll find appealing at 35. Time is such a thing that makes a difference on more occasions than one. Believe whatever you want to believe, the heart of a person will never go unnoticed.

PRAY

Big up God every time. Today, tomorrow, next week and next year. A man can't always try to do everything on his own. That is one of the fastest ways to build stress. Independence comes at a cost and a responsibility. It's called consistency. In good times and in bad times we must try and remain strong even when we know that for a time we consider ourselves a little weak. That's just what life is, an experience. Even when you think you have it all figured out sometimes and you do the most preparation, here comes life to test you and try to make you feel bad. I've lost my peace of mind already and I know what it feels like, I can't afford to lose it again. Sometimes some people see me sitting quietly paying attention to nothing important in particular and they wouldn't even know I'm saying a prayer deep down inside. The same thing that I'm running from is the same thing that one day I will have to face. I might just have to face it in a different way. Honestly I don't think anybody hopes for the worst in their lives. Generally, I feel like as people we all hope for the best., but life doesn't work like that. You've got to take it one day at a time as my father would say and trust that everything will work out how it's supposed to. You can't spend your time paying attention to people. You will lose every time.

Give Me a Chance

With Jah's blessings, I know that we will prosper. I know that We are very lucky people because we have each other. Don't listen to what the people say sometimes. Some people don't want us to be together, but they can't stop destiny if it's meant to be. You said I'm a dog a long long time ago and it hurt my feelings so much that I can't forget even after all this time. How's she gonna say that I'm a dog when I know I've been raised on some real old school type of love? I try to show her but I don't think that she understands. You always feel like someone's out to get ya. It's always your pain against mine and your feelings. I don't think you see it, or maybe you don't make the effort to see it. Maybe you've gotten comfortable being a victim for so long it feels weird when you're introduced to something different. You want someone to be there and I am. You want someone to love you and I do. I wasn't scared to show you even when there were times I second guessed if I should or not. I didn't always expect that things would go this far, I forced myself to lose the thoughts of my expectations. I instead told myself that you'd hurt me one day or that I'll hurt you and that a time will come when we'll eventually forget about each other. I'd be lying if I told you that I expected to do everything that we did and have as much fun as we've had. I'm happy with our life. You make me find myself at a loss for words a lot more than I'd like to admit. At the same time you make me think about things I would've never thought about if it wasn't for you. You have a beautiful energy that's unmatched and I'm not looking anywhere else to see if I can find something better. I just hope you know that it makes me feel good when you say that I make you feel safe and secure in my arms. I would never want to put you in harm's way. I'd never want to stress your head. I hope you know I'm willing to take the time to be patient so that I could understand everything that I need to be the perfect man.

I WANNA MAKE YOU A BETTER WOMAN.

I know that you can handle everything by yourself. I already know that you are an independent person. It's admirable. The world throws stones in her direction but she turns them into building blocks and keeps stepping. What more are they going to say? They already said everything that they possibly could to try and tear you down. Someone that's special, someone that's going places. That's who you are. I wonder when you smile, what it is that you are thinking. Is there something that you are hiding? What's the purpose of me being in your life if you don't feel safe? I don't want to be in your life just for one thing only. I've learned that there's more to who you are than that. How could I be selfish and let a good thing go to waste when I know that it's not easy to find someone like you? Every chance that she gets, she holds onto me in a special way as if she's never going to see me again and I can't help but notice that she has a special squeeze that I've never gotten from anyone else. I wonder where she comes from? I wonder how I'm so lucky. You make me feel like I don't want to let go. I'm not going anywhere, I'm staying right here.

Downtown Kingston

Some place I can't ever seem to forget. Even in my dreams, I still dream of this place. It's nothing like paradise and it will never be. The weather is perfect at least, but there's no beach nearby to enjoy the heat. The trees and industrial buildings give a little shade, but at the same time the natural breeze finds it hard to pass through. When I say mama where are you? Mama is some place in town. I always admire how she navigates such a busy spot with ease. People going here, and people going there. Then there's some people who are just sitting around, watching people and life go by, and you'll find that they will do that for years to come.

As a visitor, your spirit will be introduced to a strong burst of vibes and big energy. It can make some feel nervous, and some may feel just right at home.

A country bus loads up for Montego bay, and Ocho Rios as a crowd of people swarm it. Hefty luggage, food from vendors and mom's with their eager children standing in-front of them waiting to get in for the two hour ride across the island. Today it misses me, but usually I would've been among the crowd waiting to get in just like everyone else.

As that happens, every passing second a car, truck or bus contributes to the boisterous environment by blasting the latest reggae and trendy dancehall songs that the people admire. The vendors at their stalls and the people walking past find it hard not to dance and sing along. This adds a vibe to the overall energy of the environment and downtown Kingston, just wouldn't be downtown without that.

Everything's on sale and everyone who's marketing is getting a sale. I remember just not too long ago when I got my first job and received that first paycheck around Christmas time of how I was here downtown shopping to buy gifts for mom, sis and little brother and got lost in the world of discounts that everyone wanted to give. This is the place for that.

An American Airlines jet soars over more times than anyone will ever care to remember, but every now and then our curiosity strikes up a conversation and we ponder where that flight may be coming from.

Atlanta, DC or Los Angeles. Everyone wants to come into Kingston City.

EVEN WHEN IT AIN'T SUNNY.

Even if it ain't sunny I ain't complaining. I'm gonna go out there and smile, spread the love and share the happiness. Can't nobody steal my joy no matter who it is? Walk right out that door, your bad energy is not welcomed here anymore. I'm gonna smile. I'm gonna try to enjoy myself. I will have the best day today and I will not let the people who look down on me disturb the peace of mind that I've been searching for so long. I will take the bad and make it into something good. I will motivate myself as well as others. I don't need to get a million things done today. I just need to take care of what I need to. I don't need to compare myself to someone else. That part of my life is already over. There's no one I'd rather be but me. What's going on behind closed doors people don't always talk about? I know that my God is good and he works things out. Even if it ain't sunny I'm not complaining. Give me the rain, let my mind, soul and body be drenched. Let me feel uncomfortable. Let it soak all in that moment and let me embrace it for what it is. I know that the sun will shine again one day. As I walk on the road of life I understand why they say the journey is not for the weak. It takes a wholehearted commitment to be the best version of yourself and the people who look down on you will not help you, so their words shouldn't matter. I know I have to grow as a person, it takes time. I know that for as much as I grow as a person I will never be perfect. So no longer will making a mistake bother me. I expect it, learn from it and move past it because it doesn't define who I am. I'm allowed to be a better person in spite of my mistakes. A lot of times I'm just trying to find the answers for things that I haven't quite figured out yet. However, I know who I am. That's why it bothers me so much when they try to tell me what they think about who I am. I feel like nobody asked you in particular, and if you don't like me so what? I expected it. I took the positives out of it and I will move on. I've learned that I don't need every reason to fight. Life is life and people are just people. I've learned to safeguard my peace of mind. My mental health cannot be compared to silver and gold. How am I living as a person and what am I doing? Am I learning or am I just complaining? Completely missing the simplicity of the beautiful struggle that we call life? For how long would I let the people of this world who look down on me and ruin my smile? Even if it ain't sunny I ain't complaining.

www.ingramcontent.com/pod-product-compliance
Lightning Source LLC
Chambersburg PA
CBHW052337150726

47998CB00018B/2345